ABORIGINAL PEN

The Other Side of Ownership

Is Ownership the Answer Or is There a Better Way?

This book was professionally typeset on Reedsy.
Find out more at reedsy.com

Contents

1 Introduction   1

2 Game On   3

3 Ownership and Control Defined   4

4 Control Freak   7

5 Determine the Best Fit for You   10

6 Critical Thinking   12

7 Mental Health   15

8 Privacy   17

9 Lawsuit Protection   18

10 Let Them Eat Taxes   21

11 Resources   24

1

Introduction

I want to congratulate you on your journey for continued intelligence,knowledge,and information that can be beneficial in your life choices going forward. I am super excited about the information that is in this book because it is definitely something that is not taught in the formal educational systems today and it has been a game changer in my life as well. I commend you on your quest. Although this book is not the end all when it comes to this type of information, it is a start. Big things come in small packages. The information compiled in these pages is no exception. We all have been taught from a very young age that the utopia of success and status in this life is ownership. Owning a house, car, business, art, and stocks is the perceived blueprint for stability and clout if you are keeping up with the Jones'. Yes, it seems that materialism is the true barometer of success and prosperity on this earth. What if I told you that there is another way? You do not have to own anything. With the title of this book being." The Other Side of Ownership", what is on the other side? To really see this you must look away from all the materialism and begin to use your mind. The other side of owning is controlling. The purpose of this book is to give insight and intelligence on the control side of life. Enjoy and more importantly consider the alternative.

2

Game On

The title of this short chapter is "Game On" because literally the game is always on. The questions are do you realize you are in a game and do you know how to play it? This book for the most part was written to enlighten you and to give you intelligence on the above questions. The word "game" will be mentioned quite often in this book. Why? Because you are in the game right now. Some call it the Game of Life and know that it comes with rules. There is always a way around anything. Come up with creative ways to conquer the game or you continue to go around the game board your whole life being the victim instead of the victor. The question to you is are you winning? The first step is to realize that you are in a game. Are you the hamster on a wheel? Or are you making the contracts and getting the deals. That subject is a book for another day. Monopoly is one of the greatest games ever created that gave great insight and game play examples on winning actions and strategies. Then came the great businessman and author who created the 'Cash Flow" board game. Now I have my own game I created in real time and I am winning. You should consider creating your own game that you control.

3

Ownership and Control Defined

Before we can really understand the information in this book, we must have an understanding of the words up for discussion. The words ownership and control must be defined. Ownership has been set as the gold standard and is very popular in the society of the successful today. It seems as if the more relevant people today own more material things than someone who owns nothing and is dependent on other means for sustenance from the government. I would argue not to allow your self worth to be equated to your net worth.

Ownership is a favorite word used by the game today. We have been programmed to own. The benchmark for today is to own as much as you can within your lifetime, but at what expense? Ownership is playing by the game's rules. I don't want to play by the game's rules. One can never get ahead that way. I want the cheat codes or what is commonly known today as loop holds. A statement that must be considered is this, if you are not cheating then you are not trying. I have been told from a very young age to try my best at any and everything I do. Some of you reading this now may have the same sentiments.

Merriam-Webster dictionary defines an owner as someone who owns something. A person who has legal or rightful title to something.

Someone whom property belongs to. The legal and rightful title to something is an owner and ownership is " the state, relation, or fact of being an owner." according to the Merriam-Webster dictionary.

Ownership is fools gold because at the end of the day you are still being controlled. Someone else is pulling the strings and you ,as the owner, are the puppet. The Game makes you think you have control by way of ownership. Home ownership is a very popular push in the status game today. So you think you own your home? According to nolo.com if you as a homeowner were behind on your hoa payments but current on your mortgage payments can the hoa foreclose on the home that you own. The short answer is yes. It is quite possible that you will be foreclosed on. So much for ownership and all that equity. Staying on the housing subject of ownership, what happens if you can not afford to pay the property taxes on your home that you own? Laws differ from state to state, but for the sake of this book the great state of Texas will be used as our example. Everything is big in Texas! In the state of Texas according to afic.org, a taxing authority is allowed to begin foreclosure actions at any point after the homeowners taxes become delinquent. Do your homework on delinquency. This next example is not meant to trigger anyone but is very important for awareness purposes. Your children may be under your care and ownership but the minute that some kind of abuse is reported about you with your children then the system will swoop in and remove your children from you. Research child protective services and their power in your state. You may have ownership of your children but you will quickly find out that it is the state that has control. Learn from this!

Merriam-Webster dictionary defines control as " to exercise restraining or directing influence over: regulate" and "to have power over: rule". To regulate and rule is the definition of control according to Webster. When you are in control, you have the ability to manage and delegate who will do what and when. You are the facilitator of the entity or business.

You may not know anything about the restaurant business, but can hire someone who does. Remember you are the manager. Control is how the kings and queens live. They do not own anything but they manage and rule everything. Do your homework on the monarchy in the United Kingdom.

4

Control Freak

One thing that will be written about me in my story will be that I did it my way. If Burger King and Frank Sinatra can have it their way, then so can I. Those who create win and those who coalesce never get ahead. Again just the hamster on a wheel. Nelson Rockefeller said, "The secret to success is to own nothing, but control everything." This statement may be shocking and foreign to some because it is polar opposite of the popular ownership push today. In fact, do you remember at any time in your formal education the statement that Nelson Rockefeller quoted above taught in school? The Rockefeller name is well known throughout the world and indeed is synonymous with wealth and success. Can the same be said for all those who have embraced ownership? You decide! This book was written to discuss the other side, "Control". Control is the name to win the game. This is why I am a control freak. Information is indeed power. Most have been hoodwinked and led astray by the formal education of the game today. It is time to unlearn so that the relearning can begin. It is never too late to become a control freak. It can begin right now. Ask yourself everyday when you wake up what can you learn today. Everyday is a day to learn something new!

The key to doing anything worthwhile in the game is working hard or at least that is what is echoed all around your surroundings. Your grandmother, father, mother, teachers, and friends are all telling you to put in sweat equity to make something of yourself in the world. Do some case studies on some hard workers you are familiar with and note how sweat equity worked out for them. Did they leave a legacy of wealth? Were they healthy? Did they transition at a ripe old age? The game will tell you to go to school, work hard, get a job, buy a house, and get a car because they want you to be a good little worker bee for the hive (shout out to Robert Kiyosaki). There may be many who are very happy and content with this lifestyle and I take my hat off to them. The object of this book is to present the other side of hard work so that an intelligent decision can be made when presented with different options. There are many reasons to make the case for why working hard is important. Becomingminimalist.com gives the argument for why hard work is necessary. Hard work brings joy and happiness to the individual and leads to a fulfilling life. When you do the best you can to accomplish the most you can is the example of a rewarding life according to becomingminimalist.com. Working hard is a great example for your children, benefits the society, and keeps your life occupied with important matters according to becomingminimalist.com. If these traits resonate with you then own it, but I would argue that there is more to life than the opinions stated above.

The other side of hard work is smart work. When I think of working smart, the first word that comes to mind is efficiency. The goal is to get the same work done but in a creative or simplistic way utilizing less energy so that other goals and objectives can be accomplished in the same amount of time. It has been said that time is your greatest asset, if that is the case then working smarter would give more time back to you than working hard. Let's examine the stress factor. Working smart lessens the feeling of being inundated with tasks thus giving you the ability to approach your task with a clear head. Stress levels would indeed decrease if a person had the ability to produce more with less effort. One would argue that A.I. will benefit humanity by reducing stress levels in humans by being able to produce more with less effort. The push back on that would be that humans would be under more stress because the A.I. would leave them jobless. A whole book can be written on this topic. I have digressed from the subject a little so now we will put the train back on the track. Stress will be discussed more in the mental health chapter. As a control freak,you create the environment that is best for you. This is not a one size fits all solution. Experience ownership and control then see what environment best suits you. Do not just settle for being shoved in a category and told to work hard and make the best of it. That is insanity and not smart!

5

Determine the Best Fit for You

Every Great person has a great teacher. This is one of the biggest action steps that must be taken if you desire to create your own game or just continue to be a gamer in this never ending rat race. In your journey you must seek out those who have already reached the pinnacle of where you want to go. For me it was my thinking that I did not want to be in the life with my family, loved ones, and friends if I could not do anything for them. This is one of the big reasons why this book was penned.

Information is power! This is another reason why this book was written. The purpose of the game is to keep you playing the game. On the other hand, the purpose of this book is to help each and every individual who reads this book find their purpose. Playing by the game's rules will prevent you from finding your purpose. You become preoccupied with bills and overtime. You are too tired to even think about your purpose when you return home from working 9 to 5. Play your game by your rules. There is much to offer structurally and strategically if given the right information and intelligence. Do you want to be an owner with all the responsibilities that come with it, good, bad, and indifferent? Does being a control freak suit you? You are managing entities in the background without the fanfare of ownership but all the benefits. Proper information will be a great asset in helping you make an informed decision. The right information will likely not come from the traditional forms of education. Research on your part will be required.

In order to understand what is best for you it is very important to understand you first. The "you education" has truly been neglected or should i say ignored today. The game only wants you to do what is best for the game and that means being the best worker bee that you can be for the hive. Do you really know yourself? How much do you know about yourself? In order to know what is best for you, it is important to know you! Remember to question everything. How do you begin to know yourself? Google and Alexia will not be able to help you with this question. You have a purpose and once you know your purpose then you can develop your plan. I will say again " YOU HAVE A PURPOSE". The birth chart is the beginning to understanding you. There you will find the attributes that will reflect your nature or design. The good, the bad and the ugly! You came into this existence on a particular day and at a certain time for a reason. There are people in this world who received years and years of education in a particular field of study, because that was the thing to do or they wanted to please their parents. Only to realize that they are not happy and dislike what they do. What a terrible way to live. Multiply this example by hundreds if not thousands or millions,unfortunately. When it comes to you it is important to be proactive and not reactive. Another reason this book was written is to bring balance to you when it comes to decision making. Before making a decision having all the facts available and a healthy examination of all sides is important.

6

Critical Thinking

Critical thinking is the ability to be able to create. Your creative ideals, thoughts, ect. You learn to think for yourself. This is the first classroom and the most important education. Many have skipped this class and have gone right into the game's programming. Just remember, it is never too late to begin to think for yourself. This may seem like common sense but common sense is not all too common anymore. Self control may seem like a play on words but it plays a major role in your preservation and ability to think as an individual. Control yourself!

When you know better you will do better. Google millionaires that have no formal education? You may be surprised. It is time to reverse engineer what the game has conditioned you to believe is true.

The game is meant to be sold, not told. This is why you pay so much for the game's conditioning called education. Education is expensive in two ways, monetary and time consumption. Some students spend 4,6,8, and even 10 plus years in college, grad school, or doctorate programs. This is time that will not be returned to you. The expenses on these programs are more than unreasonable as well. Student loan debt continues to increase at unsustainable levels. Most students spend a majority of their careers paying off their student loan debt. Think about what you are consuming with your time. Yes time! Have you ever heard of the saying, time is money? I would argue that time is even more valuable than money. Wake up and invest in "self" education so that you can get your time back and keep your money instead of giving a majority of it away in the game's systems.

The game keeps you preoccupied with entertainment. Entertainment is a system that the game uses to keep you distracted. According to marketingcharts.com, the top three past month activities for American adults are listening to music 88%(radio,screaming,and records), watching streaming tv 80%(Netflix or Hulu), and watching short term videos 76%(Tiktok and Youtube). Wow! These are very interesting numbers and activities. Notice that American adults are listening and looking at what is being sold to them by the game with a goal to keep them away from things that really matter. The entertainment described above is what I would argue is shaping your behavior if not thinking for you as well.

Preoccupy yourself with yourself. Yes, make a conscious decision to invest in yourself. Investing in yourself will require you to think about you in a critical way. Look at how the game is played. The game's agenda is to keep your mind set in the past or in the future. If this is accomplished then it would be almost possible for you to think in the present. The present is just that, a gift. If you were given a gift today would you refuse it? Probably not! Think about all the people in the world that are rejecting their gift because they refuse to live and focus on the now. They refuse to critically think for themselves and just allow entertainment to keep them in their past or a projected future somewhere. I want you to critically think about this statement. When your projected future comes. It will be in real time, the present. As far back as you can go in the past, you can never change the occurrences. Don't stay in replay mode. Learn from the occurrences of the past and apply the lessons to your present. The game is draining you of your talents and abilities to make you a host of whatever it wants to promote. It is high time for you to become your own Don King. Promote yourself. Make it a point to put your attention on yourself. One of the game's objectives is to grab your attention. The solution is to take what the game meant to be a distraction and use it for your benefit. Critical thinking will have you reverse engineer what you have been conditioned to believe is true according to the environmental standard.

Following the rules of the game versus making your own rules and creating your own game that you control is a decision that only you can make for yourself. Control is key because if you don't control you are being controlled whether you know it or not. It is funny how this whole monopoly game is set up. If you are still indecisive about ownership versus control then consider that when you came into this world you did not own anything and guess what when you leave this world there is nothing that you will take with you. With that being said, What should you be owning now? In my opinion, absolutely nothing! One reason it is important to think for yourself is because the game's goal is to think for you whether you believe it or not. Amazon and Alexia are telling you what you need and information sources that are best for you. Question everything. Never stop learning. When questioning is ceased the learning stops.

7

Mental Health

The PPP Plan: Happy equals Peace of Mind, Protection, and Privacy in my opinion. Thus, the PPP formula. Follow this equation and it will change your mental situation. Think about how many so-called successful people that own a lot of material things and wealth are very unhappy. It begs the question, does material wealth make you happy? The PPP Plan has nothing to do with exterior factors (material) or outside forces, it is all about the internal self because the force is within you. It is time to be selfish and learn to love yourself in a real way.

Time to do some spring cleaning of your internals. Does anyone remember spring cleaning growing up as a child? This is when all the old things went in the trash can to make room for the new things coming. Yes, out with the old and in with the new. There can be a lot of baggage that we carry during our lifetime that needs to be thrown in the bin. It is detrimental to your mental and physical health if you don't. The baggage can cloud your judgment thus affecting your decision making process. According to a Penn State study, if the baggage will not cloud your decision making process then it may be related to the prescription drugs usage. The study states that Americans will spend half their lives taking prescription drugs. Enough said! It seems if you are not in control then you are definitely being controlled. This study is an example of a controlling vehicle,medicine. It is quite difficult to have some form of peace of mind when your body is full of prescription drugs.

According to WedMed seventy-five percent to ninety percent of all visits to the doctors office are for stress-related issues and complaints. Stress is a big player in problems such as depression,anxiety, asthma, arthritis, skin issues, diabetes, heart problems, high blood pressure and headaches just to name a few. As you can see your decision to choose a life of ownership or controlling everything but owning nothing is huge. It could even be a matter of life and death. Your mental health is indeed your wealth. What environment will you settle for?

Do worry about a thing! According to webmd, worry is defined as being overly concerned and feeling uneasy about a problem or situation. Worry only about the things that are in your control, not the things that are not in your control. Worrying can also lead to anxiety if not addressed properly. Daily life can also be altered in the form of your appetite, sleep, lifestyle habits, relationships, and job performance because of worrying. In a recent survey on cnbc.com, a little more than three in four Americans which is 77% are feeling anxious about their financial situation according to a survey done by capital one and the decision lab. Decision time for you will be to choose which scenario will be best for you that will lessen your worry meter ownership or control. The solution for your mental awareness is to remember "what will be, will be!". Sometimes we make things that are so simple and difficult and vice versa. Mental Health is real! Self love is the best love.

8

Privacy

If you think your privacy is secured just google your name on the internet. In this day and age we are in now, privacy is the last line of defense. The last stand! It is often said that this existence is about give and take. This game is often taking and almost never giving so the mission statement for the individual would be to go get it. Go get your privacy because the game is definitely desiring to take your privacy from you. Look around you there are many examples. Do you see them? More importantly, what are you going to do about it? People pay a lot of money for privacy these days in this give and take society we are in. If you ask the right questions about privacy to the right people, you will get the best answer. There are many strategies and ways to structure your privacy on the personal and professional sides as owners and controllers of business entities. This book is meant to point you in alternative directions. It is your responsibility to access and research the best options when it refers to privacy.

9

Lawsuit Protection

In boxing, before a fight takes place the referee will tell both fighters at the center of the ring to protect yourself at all times. Some may consider this life as not only a game but a fight as well. I recall the famous line in the movie The Color Purple, "All my life I had to fight '', where Oprah Winfrey says this line as the character Sophia in the movie. The question in this chapter is which is the best vehicle to choose for protection, being an owner or having the control. Let's get to the point of this chapter. Which is the best position when it comes to protection, ownership or control? When we are talking about protection we are talking about lawsuit protection. It would be a shame to have the wonderful business that you worked so hard on, from just an idea in your head, to be taken away from you because you were knocked out by a lawsuit. As an owner of a business it would be wise to get your boxing gloves on because in a typical year businesses spend 1.2 million dollars on average fighting lawsuits according to uschamber.com. As an owner the law will come after you and your businesses. The Controller does not own anything,they only manage businesses and entities. If the controller does not own anything, what is there for the law to take? Absolutely nothing! Nothing from nothing will leave you with nothing.

What a great strategy for the controller. An owner has a legal title to something so in the eyes of the law the owner is liable.

Do your own research when it comes to a business/owner involved in a lawsuit, have a conversion with a local attorney in your community that is an experienced litigator. Their response may be similar to this. On average only 1% of court cases go to trial. The other 99% of court cases are settled outside of the courtroom. There are several reasons for this but for the benefit of this small book and time we will only examine a few. Court cases are settled very quickly if it is determined that only the insurance money will be rewarded or if it is felt like the court case is on the fence and not a slam dunk case. In the determination process, attorneys will attempt to break the corporate veil of your LLC, C or S corp, and partnership. If your entity that is registered to your state is out of compliance then the veil has been broken. An example would be not having your operating argument up to date. This example is low hanging fruit for attorneys because most owners are not compliant with their state requirements for their registered entities to date. Another determination strategy is to sue the owner. Yes, another worry of an owner is a personal lawsuit and loss of everything of value they own. This makes Nelson Rockefeller's statement about owning nothing and controlling everything worth studying. This idea is counter intuitive to the game. Indeed, whatever the game is doing or promoting I would do the opposite.

There are entities, vehicles, structures, and provisions that are outside the reach of statutory law. Common law is that other side. If you do not want to own then control through common law this is a great strategy for you. Common law deals with control through contracts. Common law teaching in law schools stopped around the year of 1978. It may be difficult to find an attorney that practices or that is knowledgeable about common law. Jurisdiction is going to be a key question to ask when it comes to whether you desire ownership or control for yourself as you mind your business. If this sparked your attention, then consider a common law trust as the entity for you to control. Much more could be said but for the sake of time we will end it here. Do your own research and remember to question everything.

10

Let Them Eat Taxes

The poor and working class Americans pay higher payroll tax rates than the rich according to american progress.org. This fact may be unbelievable to some but it is definitely true. This is how the game is played even though it may not seem fair to most who read this book. The real question is what are you going to do about it if anything? Does ownership give you an advantage when it comes to giving away your hard earned money in the form of taxes or is the controller in a better position when it comes to tax liabilities? Let's answer a question with a question. What are the rich and wealthy doing? The key to getting a clear and concise answer is to follow the money. Are a majority of the rich owners or controllers? That is the million dollar question and puts you on a road map to multiple roads of solutions.

There are 9 states in the U.S. that do not have a state income tax: Alaska, Florida, Nevada, New Hampshire, Texas, Tennessee, South Dakota, Washington, and Wyoming according to NerdWallet.com. Moved to one of these states to avoid state taxes and save money. Not so fast! On the surface this may sound like a great strategy to avoid paying taxes if you live in one of the 9 states named. On the other hand,be mindful of higher cost of living and other taxes in the named states so do your research before reacting.

The game has rules for tax avoidance but tax evasion is against the law. Taking advantage of the U.S. tax code to lower your income taxes is not against the law or using asset protection vehicles like properly constructed trust to reduce your tax liability is not breaking the law. The author of the book is not a financial advisor or CPA and I did not stay at a Holiday Inn last night. On the other hand, I have an awesome financial planning team behind me from specialized CPA's, IRS enrolled tax preparers, and an estate planning mentor that I am quite happy to pay for their guidance, intelligence, and experience. I would encourage you all to do the same because at the end of the day it is not what you know but who you know. One must remember the game will be sold and not told. The reason why I choose to write this book and give you some game on the game is because I truly do care, and I am passionate about everyone winning. The intelligence required to win and manipulate the game in your favor is not free. You will have to pay for it. Freedom however you see it is not free. It must be paid for. For those who may be on the fence or in the cheap seats understand this, if you don't pay now you will pay later. The cookie cutter tax advice I received from the tax companies on every corner in my neighborhood did not give me the advice that I needed to win the game. Their advice only kept me going around the game board. I guess you get what you pay for. This book is not intended to go deep into the woods when it comes to taxes but it is intended to show you the other side to taxes and to assist with ideals and resources that can aid in successful tax seasons going forward. Yes! The IRS and Taxes can be your best friends.

The tax code(Internal Revenue Code) just keeps getting longer and longer according to Pew Research Center. What is the reason? Just using critical thinking, one may say there is a need to write more tax code to get more tax dollars from the taxpayers. You decide. A whole book or even volumes of books can be written on taxes.

Common Tax breaks for the business owner. Qualified business income, Marketing and advertising materials and services, Rent on an office or storefront, Office supplies, and Business related travel and meals. These are just a few of the tax deductions that can be taken advantage of as a business owner.

As one controlling a vehicle or entity it is a whole new world when it comes to the irs tax code and how much payment if any is given to the irs. There are multiple ways and strategies that a controller can take based upon which vehicle the controller selects. These vehicles or entities include but are not limited to LLC's, C and S Corps, Partnerships, and Trust. There are an unlimited amount of strategies that can be created for the controller to avoid taxes based upon the IRS tax code. Deferral strategy through a properly structured trust is worth examining. You do not have to take my words for it. Set up a consultation with the tax specialist and they will tell you the same thing. Ask them how you can become a controller, Nelson Rockefeller style? Not a W2 worker nor Owner but a Controller. Remember to question everything! If you do not ask the right question to the right person you can never get the right answer!

11

Resources

https://advocacy.sba.gov/2022/11/08/small-business-facts/

https://sbnonline.com/article/ownership-vs-control-using-charitabl
e-strategies-in-business-succession-planning-can-help-you-avoid
-large-contributions-to-uncle-sam/#:~:text=Ownership%20of%20
assets%20carries%20with,capital%20gain%20and%20estate%20tax
es.

https://www.merriam-webster.com/dictionary/owner

https://www.merriam-webster.com/dictionary/control

https://www.nolo.com/legal-encyclopedia/im-behind-hoa-dues-mo
rtgage-can-the-hoa-foreclose.html

https://afic.co/blog/how-long-can-you-be-delinquent-on-your-pro
perty-taxes-in-texas

https://onlinemba.wsu.edu/blog/benefits-of-owning-your-own-bus

iness

https://www.uschamber.com/lawsuits/arbitration/liability-lawsuits-business-guide

https://www.pewresearch.org/short-reads/2024/04/09/7-facts-abou t-americans-and-taxes/

https://www.americanprogress.org/article/5-little-known-facts-abo ut-taxes-and-inequality-in-america/

https://www.nerdwallet.com/article/taxes/states-with-no-income-t ax

https://www.findlaw.com/tax/tax-problems-audits/famous-tax-eva sion-cases.html

https://www.irs.gov/individuals/tax-withholding-estimator

https://www.brainyquote.com/quotes/nelson_rockefeller_170273

https://www.becomingminimalist.com/work-hard/

https://www.psu.edu/news/research/story/americans-will-spend-ha lf-their-lives-taking-prescription-drugs-study-finds/?utm_source =substack&utm_medium=email

https://www.webmd.com/balance/stress-management/effects-of-str ess-on-your-body

https://www.webmd.com/balance/how-worrying-affects-your-body

https://www.cnbc.com/select/how-to-take-control-of-your-finance
s/

https://www.marketingcharts.com/industries/media-and-entertain
ment-231730